W9-BZH-746

PRESIDENTIAL
CAMPAIGN

PRESIDENTIAL CAMPAIGN

Thomas R. Raber

Lerner Publications Company
Minneapolis

The photo on page two shows President Ronald Reagan speaking at the U.S. Capitol during his inaugural ceremony.

Front cover photograph: Courtesy of Independent Picture Service
Back cover photograph: ISP Photo by Arnold Sachs

Cover illustration by Stephen Clement

Copyright © 1988 by Lerner Publications Company

Library of Congress Cataloging—in—Publication Data

Raber, Thomas R.
    Presidential campaign/Thomas R. Raber.
        p.   cm.
    Bibliography: p.
    Includes index.
    Summary: Examines the political campaigns of American presidents
throughout history.
    ISBN 0-8225-1750-7 (lib. bdg.)
    1. Presidents—United States—Election—Juvenile literature.
2. Electioneering—United States—Juvenile literature.
[1. Presidents—Election. 2. Politics, Practical.] I. Title.
JK524.R33 1988
324.973—dc19   88-22688
                                                             CIP
                                                              AC

Manufactured in the United States of America

1 2 3 4 5 6 7 8 9 10 97 96 95 94 93 92 90 91 89 88

Contents

President Franklin D. Roosevelt and his wife, Eleanor, wave happily to the crowds and cameras

1

Presidential Ambition

"Wouldn't you be president if you could?" Franklin D. Roosevelt once asked a friend. "Wouldn't anybody?"

President Roosevelt must have thought it was a great job. He held the office longer than anyone, successfully campaigning for the presidency four times and living in the White House 13 years, from 1933 until his death in April 1945.

He was the only president to serve more than two terms and he will be the last. The United States' first president, George Washington, had declined to run for a third term in 1796 and it had become an unwritten rule that no president should serve more than two terms. Roosevelt broke that 144-year-old tradition when he ran for a third term in 1940. Shortly after his death, the 22d Amendment to the Constitution was adopted, limiting presidents to no more than two consecutive terms.

More than most presidents, Roosevelt widely used the powers of the office. His **administration**—a word that describes a president's full staff of workers — led the nation through the Great Depression of the 1930s. This was a time when millions of Americans were poor, or were earning far less money than they had in the past.

Roosevelt's administration also:
♦ Decided that the United States would enter World War II. Before he died, Roosevelt was able to see America begin to bring an end to the long conflict.

- Selected justices to the United States Supreme Court. These were lifetime appointees whose legal decisions would be followed by generations of Americans.
- Developed widespread social programs, such as Social Security, that operate to this day.

Roosevelt won his elections by some of the largest margins in history. He is remembered as one of the United States' most effective presidents. People named their children after him, and when he died people wept.

But was it worth it? Did his power and popularity make up for the pressure of making difficult choices,

This cartoon shows Roosevelt's power over the news, as a room full of reporters sits waiting anxiously for his every word.

knowing that millions of people would be affected by what he did and said?

Apparently, some other presidents did not think so. Listen to this comment from the 1790s: "I would rather be in my grave than in the presidency." Can you guess the speaker?

It was George Washington, the "Father of Our Country." In 1789 he took on a job no one ever had held before, one that no one knew exactly how to describe.

He soon found the presidency to be overwhelming, and he was not alone for long in his feelings. Washington's successor in office, John Adams, was equally unsettled about his term as chief executive. "No man who ever held the office of president would congratulate a friend on obtaining it," Adams said. "He will make one man ungrateful and 100 men his enemies for every office he can bestow."

Thomas Jefferson, the nation's third president, once called the office nothing but "splendid misery." When he left the White House in 1808, he heaved a sigh of relief.

"Never did a prisoner released from his chains feel such relief as I shall on shaking off the shackles of power," Jefferson said.

Even Abraham Lincoln, remembered as one of America's most patient and effective presidents, felt pressure from the job. Soon after taking charge, Lincoln wrote to a friend, "I feel like the man who was tarred and feathered and ridden out of town on a rail."

In 1865, Lincoln's face showed the strain of five years of the presidency.

A century later, John F. Kennedy felt the same pressures. Even though he had seen naval combat during World War II, served in the U.S. Senate, survived a life-threatening kidney condition and a painful back problem, just one year as president moved him to say, "There is no experience you can get that possibly can prepare you adequately for the presidency."

A president's duties are many. The Constitution makes it a president's responsibility to be commander-in-chief of the armed forces. That means the president is the ultimate boss of American soldiers. The president also is responsible for discussing treaties and other agreements with foreign countries. Further, the president is empowered to select judges for the U.S. Supreme Court. This task is important because members of the Supreme Court interpret how strictly the laws of the country may be applied.

George Washington and his cabinet: (left to right) George Washington; Henry Knox, Secretary of War; Alexander Hamilton, Secretary of the Treasury; Thomas Jefferson, Secretary of State; and Edmund Randolph, Attorney General.

The president is helped in making decisions by a staff called a **cabinet**. These are the most important people in a president's administration. They are selected by the president to take care of the country's major business. The authority to choose a cabinet is one of a president's important powers.

The Constitution limits the power of presidents, however, so that presidents must listen to the opinions of people who might disagree with them. The laws or agreements a president wants to adopt must be voted on by members of Congress, who may reject the president's plans.

When presidents disagree with a plan that Congress has approved, however, they can reject Congress' plan by **vetoing** the measure. The word **veto** comes from a Latin word meaning "forbid." Congress can still pass a measure that has been vetoed, but only if at least two-thirds of its members vote to override the president's wishes.

No matter the burdens, there *is* glory in the job, and many see it as the ultimate personal challenge. What the president says and does affects people far beyond the borders of the United States, making the presidency a position in which someone can make an important difference in history.

Today, students all over the world still study the political ideas of Thomas Jefferson. Abraham Lincoln is widely remembered for his wise decisions during the time of the Civil War, when Americans were at war with other Americans. And Harry Truman is famous for having the courage to speak his mind, even when many disagreed with him.

Franklin D. Roosevelt asked the question, "Wouldn't you be president if you could?"

Would you?

Becoming president is difficult. There's no one way to get to the White House, and by any route it's a tough course to travel. It takes ambition, support, money, stamina, the ability to make people like and trust you, and no small amount of luck. And often, being qualified to be president is not enough. The person who becomes president may simply be the one who mounts the best presidential campaign.

Theodore Roosevelt's competitiveness, his record in the Spanish-American War, and his family background all helped him reach the presidency.

2

Presidential Material

In February 1912, former President Theodore Roosevelt announced his plan to challenge President William Taft for the Republican party nomination. A political **party** is a group of people organized together to try to direct what the government does, and the Republican party is one such group.

Roosevelt knew that when a boxer or wrestler accepted a challenge to fight in the 1800s, he did so by tossing his hat into the ring. It was a show of a willingness to fight, like telling someone, "Let's step outside." Passing through Cleveland, Ohio, Roosevelt told a reporter, "My hat's in the ring."

Having the desire to be president is not the same as having the required tools to get to the White House. A successful candidate requires a blend of good looks, humor, speaking ability, popular ideas, and an educational and family background that voters trust. And no candidate fits the mold perfectly, because there is no mold. Even when a candidate seems qualified in many ways, something can turn up to work against the candidate.

♦ In 1944, Republican candidate Thomas E. Dewey suffered a setback when news cameras snapped his picture from the side of the stage while he spoke. The photos revealed him standing on two cardboard cartons in order to reach the microphone. The question arose: Was Dewey too short to look "presidential"?

♦ In 1984, California Senator Alan Cranston tried briefly to run for president. At age 68, he was younger than then-President Ronald Reagan. But Cranston was bald, with white sideburns and an unglamorous appearance, while President Reagan had a full head of hair and the charm of a movie actor. The question arose: Did Cranston look too old to be "presidential"?

Today, a man as gawky as Abraham Lincoln might have trouble making it to the White House. So might a guy as heavy as William Howard Taft. Before radio and television, candidates could not be so closely examined by so many voters as modern candidates are. Today, the media give millions of voters an up-close look at every candidate.

All the Constitution requires is that a president be at least 35 years old, be born in the United States, and have lived in the United States for at least 14 years. The oldest president has been Ronald Reagan, who was 69 when he was inaugurated in 1981. The youngest has been Theodore Roosevelt, who was 42 when he became president in 1901.

Roosevelt, however, was not the youngest *elected* president. He had been vice president under William McKinley and first became president (at age 42) upon McKinley's assassination. Roosevelt later was elected to the presidency and was 46 when he was inaugurated for a

President William Howard Taft: would today's voters choose a man who weighed so much as president?

Ulysses S. Grant (standing, in hat) with his staff at Army headquarters. The voters knew Grant could lead people because of his record in the Civil War.

second term. But in 1961, John F. Kennedy was 43 when he took office—the youngest person ever *elected* president.

The first seven presidents as well as the ninth, William Henry Harrison, were born British. They all were born in what became the United States, but all were born before America declared its independence from Great Britain in 1776. Martin Van Buren, the eighth president, was the first who was an American from birth.

Work Experience

There is no specific training program to prepare a person for the presidency. However, some kinds of work experience seem to lead more often to the presidency.

Presidents most often have experience and training as lawyers. In fact, 25 of the first 40 presidents were trained as lawyers before entering politics.

Four presidents—George Washington, William Henry Harrison, Zachary Taylor, and Jimmy Carter—had been soldiers and farmers before they became presidents. Three—Theodore Roosevelt, Warren Harding, and John Kennedy—had been writers or journalists. Some had been solely military men, like Ulysses Grant and Dwight Eisenhower.

Andrew Johnson had been a tailor, Herbert Hoover a mining engineer, Lyndon Johnson a teacher, and Harry Truman a clothing salesman. Ronald Reagan had been an actor and James Garfield had been a lay minister with the Disciples of Christ.

15

Most presidential candidates have had some experience in politics. They may have been a state governor, like Jimmy Carter from Georgia, Theodore Roosevelt from New York, or Ronald Reagan from California. They may have been a U.S. Representative, like Gerald Ford from Michigan, or a U.S. Senator, like John F. Kennedy from Massachusetts. Or they may have been a government official, like William Taft, who had held the title of secretary of war.

Early in United States history, the office of secretary of state was a stepping-stone to the presidency. The secretary of state is the cabinet officer in charge of making political agreements with foreign nations. In those days, the secretary of state was considered the top cabinet officer and the second in power to the president. Thomas Jefferson, James Madison, James Monroe, and John Quincy Adams all were secretaries of state before becoming presidents.

Military leaders also were popular as candidates for a period. War heroes had the advantage of being known to voters, and a candidate who had a war record could tell voters he was experienced, loyal to the country, brave, and willing to fight for what he believed. In the first half of the 19th century, Andrew Jackson, William Henry Harrison,

Dwight D. Eisenhower (right) speaks with Prime Minister Winston Churchill of England. Eisenhower, who commanded the Allied forces in Europe during World War II, was the last military leader to be elected president.

Zachary Taylor, and Franklin Pierce all became president after having fought in the War of 1812. After the Civil War, military men such as Ulysses Grant, Rutherford Hayes, James Garfield, Benjamin Harrison, and William McKinley all became president, although Grant was the only career military man among them.

In the 20th century, Theodore Roosevelt, a leader in the Spanish-American War, and Dwight Eisenhower, the leader of American and Allied forces in Europe during World War II, each became president. But the pattern of choosing military veterans as nominees, and electing them president, is largely out of fashion now.

In an age of nuclear weapons, perhaps a military person appears "too aggressive" to voters. In addition, the American population includes fewer war veterans today. Many of the veterans of World War II and their families, who might have supported a military candidate, have died. Further, many voters were not in favor of the two most recent American wars. Military candidates who fought in Korea in the 1950s and in Vietnam in the 1960s might not be popular with voters who opposed those conflicts.

Voters today are wary of military leaders as presidents, perhaps because "war" now means "nuclear weapons" to many people.

Incumbents and Vice Presidents

Incumbent presidents are those who are in office. Incumbents generally have been considered good material to carry on with the job. Only five times has an incumbent president been denied the nomination of his party: John Tyler in 1844, Millard Fillmore in 1852, Franklin Pierce in 1856, Andrew Johnson in 1868, and Chester Arthur in 1884. All but Pierce had been vice presidents and had become president by the death of their predecessor.

Gerald Ford was sworn in as president after Richard Nixon resigned in 1974.

Being vice president can help a politician in a bid for the presidency, but it is not a sure thing. Thirteen vice presidents have gone on to become president. Nine of those became president when the president died, as Lyndon B. Johnson did when John F. Kennedy was assassinated in November 1963, or when the president resigned, as Gerald Ford did when Richard Nixon resigned in August 1974. Four who became president in this way were then nominated and elected in their own right in the next succeeding term. Only three who ran for president while still in the vice president's position were successful, however.

Only one former vice president has ever won the presidency without the boost of first taking over for a departed president *and* with the disadvantage of having been out of the vice president's office for several years. Richard Nixon served as vice president under Eisenhower from 1953 to 1961, then won the 1968 presidential election.

Personal Traits

Many voters judge candidates by how the candidates conduct their personal lives. If a candidate is trustworthy in private, these voters say, the candidate can be trusted in office. Television and radio have given voters a closer look at candidates' private lives than was possible years ago. But even before radio and television, candidates always were careful to present their best personal side to the public.

Before Warren Harding was nominated at the 1920 Republican **convention** in Chicago, party leaders called Harding into a hotel room and asked him bluntly, "Is there anything in your private life that could affect your personal integrity or harm your chances of winning if it came out? If there is, we want to know it now." Harding satisfied his questioners that it was safe to nominate him. Even so, his administration proved to be inefficient and riddled with scandal.

When Franklin Roosevelt ran for vice president in 1920 and then president in 1932, many people were unaware that Roosevelt used a wheelchair after having suffered from polio. With cooperation from the press, Roosevelt's condition was concealed and it never became an issue. Today, such a condition would almost certainly become common knowledge and be discussed as a possible disadvantage or asset to his campaign.

Scandals and accidents can hurt a campaign effort. In 1969 Senator Edward Kennedy was driving a car on Chappaquiddick Island, Massachusetts. The car went off a bridge and a female aide who was in the car with Kennedy drowned. Kennedy's explanation of the incident was doubted by some people. The incident hurt his future as a presidential hopeful. It appeared that Kennedy had been dating the aide, even though he was married. Also, some said Kennedy did not fully explain why he abandoned his car at the scene of the accident.

It seems that a spouse is an asset to a candidate, since only two presidents have been bachelors. Many

Jackie Kennedy's appeal to voters was a definite help in John Kennedy's 1960 campaign.

voters believe a candidate who is married leads a more settled life and knows the discipline of providing for a family. A candidate with a spouse also enjoys the advantage of having an effective campaigner right in the family. Many voters listen carefully to what a candidate's spouse says, believing that a spouse gives a special inside, personal view of the candidate.

Only one president, Ronald Reagan, has been divorced. Divorce used to be thought "immoral." Some voters felt that candidates who had been divorced were not as committed to their goals as were candidates who had stayed married. In 1952 and 1956, the divorced status of Senator Adlai

Stevenson of Illinois was a minor but persistent campaign issue. Dwight Eisenhower defeated Stevenson in both campaigns. Today, divorce is no longer unusual in the United States and people's attitudes about divorce have changed.

Candidates' Backgrounds

Many presidents have come from very similar backgrounds. To begin with, each president from the first to the fortieth has been of Northern European heritage. There have been none of Mediterranean, Middle-Eastern, African, or Latin American descent. Most Americans are from families that originally came from Europe. Because of their greater numbers, white people of European descent typically have had more political power than people from other backgrounds.

In addition, presidents generally have been wealthy, although in this century, Eisenhower and Ford were exceptions. Wealthy candidates can afford to spend more money for more effective campaigns than candidates with less money. They also are more likely to have wealthy friends and associates to help finance their campaigns.

Most nominees have come from states with large populations. Since 1900, New York state alone has produced Theodore Roosevelt, Woodrow Wilson, and Franklin D. Roosevelt along with several unsuccessful candidates. California has produced Presidents Nixon and Reagan, and President Lyndon B. Johnson came from Texas. The common belief is that many voters from a candidate's home state will support the candidate. A candidate from a larger state has a larger group of ready-made supporters and a boost toward victory.

Almost all candidates have been mainstream Protestant Christians. In 1928, when Alfred Smith of New York lost to Herbert Hoover, one of the main issues of the campaign was Smith's membership in the Roman Catholic church. Some voters feared that Smith would seek to impose strict Roman Catholic principles on people of differing faiths. Others feared that Smith would be controlled by the Pope.

In 1960, John Kennedy became the first Roman Catholic to be elected president, but his religion was still considered something he had to overcome in his campaign.

In 1984, Democrat Jesse Jackson, a black man, became the first member of a racial minority to challenge for the nomination of a major political party. Jackson fell short of the Democratic nomination but went on to run **independently**, or without the backing of a major party organization. Jackson's showing in the 1988 election was even stronger, and he gained enough support to be discussed for the vice presidential candidacy.

Jackson's candidacy was not the first by a black person. In 1888, Frederick Douglass became the first black man to get a vote in a party's nomination process. He got one vote on the fourth ballot at that year's Republican convention.

In 1872, Douglass had served as a **running mate** for Victoria Claflin Woodhull. He was the vice presidential candidate and Woodhull ran for president under the Equal Rights Party. Woodhull is often listed as the first woman to run for president. Woodhull and Douglass won only 1,000 votes that year, but Woodhull ran again in 1880 and 1892.

Much later, at the 1964 Republican convention, Senator Margaret Chase Smith from Maine had her name placed in nomination for president. This was the first time a woman had been up for the nomination of a major party. At the 1952 Republican convention, Smith had been suggested as the running mate

for Dwight Eisenhower, but she had declined.

In 1984, Congresswoman Geraldine Ferraro of New York became the Democratic vice presidental nominee, becoming the first woman to run on a major party's presidential **ticket**.

The Intelligence Factor

Does an intelligent person make the best presidential candidate? It may seem surprising, but extremely bright people have not done well running for president.

Adlai Stevenson, twice a Democratic candidate in the 1950s, was recognized as a witty, scholarly man. But he lost twice to Eisenhower, who showed a warmer personality and inspired more public confidence. People liked "Ike," and his success showed that becoming president requires more than having good ideas about government.

Effective presidents not only make wise decisions for the country. They also inspire people to have *confidence* in those decisions. And presidential candidates who inspire confidence in their leadership most often become president.

Dwight D. Eisenhower and his wife Mamie greet the crowds from the back of a train car on their whistle-stop campaign.

3
Campaign Rigors

One typical day during the 1984 presidential campaign, Democratic candidate Walter Mondale visited 8 southern cities in 18 hours. That same day, in a 24-hour period, Democratic candidate Jesse Jackson flew from Pittsburgh, Pennsylvania, to Madison, Wisconsin, to Milwaukee, Wisconsin, and then to New Orleans, Louisiana, in a 12-seat plane, making 5 speeches and sleeping intermittently for about 5 hours.

A presidential campaign is not a normal job. It's a 24-hour-a-day duty of smiling, shaking hands, making speeches, and showing enthusiasm at stop after stop, on an endless string of appearances at rallies, shopping centers, club meetings, and dinners. President Ronald Reagan once called it "the torture trail."

Candidates eat on the run, sleep when they can, and hope that sheer exhaustion doesn't make them say something embarrassing when the television cameras are rolling.

In 1952, General Dwight Eisenhower was campaigning as the Republican nominee on the way to becoming the country's 34th President. He traveled by railroad, conducting what was known as a "whistle-stop" campaign. In such a campaign, the candidate would speak to townspeople who gathered around the back of the train at each stop along the route. Many small towns had no train station, so people got off and boarded at the side of the tracks. Because the stop was signalled by the sound of the train's whistle, these stops became known as "whistle stops."

23

Eisenhower was good at this type of campaigning. His advisors pushed him to go at it seven days a week, even though he was getting only four hours of sleep each night. Eisenhower was a hero from the recently ended World War II. Even in the largely Democratic southern states he was so popular that, if necessary, his aides would drag him out of bed to appear on the rear platform. At one point, he said of his aides, "Are they trying to perform the feat of electing a dead man?"

The Candidate's Image

Despite the tough schedule, it is vital for presidential candidates to get their rest and appear healthy, happy, and, therefore, vigorous enough to lead the nation. The first presidents were judged almost entirely by what they were quoted as saying in newspapers. But train and air travel, and radio and television, have made modern candidates more visible to voters. To many people, a candidate's appearance is more important than what a candidate says about the issues of the day.

Talking about government can be boring and confusing, and many people do not care to listen. It is easier to judge how candidates look and speak than to judge what is on their minds. As a result, a successful campaign often has little to do with whether a candidate can offer solutions to national problems, demonstrate good judgment, or show what a responsible president he or she would make. Instead, candidates try to sell themselves to as much of the country as possible.

When people are shopping, they trust the brands they know by name, even if other brands are just as good. Campaigning serves the same purpose as an ad for a car or a breakfast cereal. It gives voters a chance to see the candidate, meet him or her, and get the feeling they know the candidate personally.

Henry Clay was a United States Senator during the mid-1800s who campaigned and lost three times for the presidency. He said that voters often expect extraordinary thoughts and actions from politicians, while at the same time expecting them to be "ordinary fellows like thee and me."

This is why voters see candidates wearing hard hats at construction sights, flipping hamburgers at fast-food restaurants, and pumping gas at quick shops. The candidates want to balance their wealthy, coat-and-tie image by appearing to be just like people everywhere. Although a candidate should look like a leader, it is also important to look like a neighbor, someone anybody could walk up and talk to.

Campaign Dangers

Campaigning is not only tiring, it can be dangerous. Candidates are constantly in crowds, speaking about government, and everywhere there are bound to be people who disagree with them.

In 1912, former Republican President Theodore Roosevelt was hit in the ribs by a gunshot on his way to make a campaign speech. Although wounded and bleeding, Roosevelt went ahead and made his speech before entering a hospital to be treated. Republican candidate Woodrow Wilson, who won the election that year and became the 28th president, put his campaign on hold until Roosevelt recovered.

In 1972, Governor George Wallace of Alabama was shot while campaigning in a shopping center in Laurel, Maryland. The shots left him partly paralyzed and confined to a wheelchair.

Robert Kennedy was shot and killed while campaigning for the Democratic nomination in 1968.

Robert (left) and John F. Kennedy were both victims of presidential politics. John was killed while president and Robert was killed while running for president.

Each of these men was attacked because of presidential politics. None was even the president. They were only candidates on the campaign trail.

25

New York newspapers predicted Charles Evans Hughes as the new president on election night 1916, but Hughes woke the next morning to find he had lost to Woodrow Wilson.

26

4

A Brief History of Campaigns

In 1916, Republican candidate Charles Evans Hughes held an early lead over Democratic President Woodrow Wilson. Hughes was a respected justice on the U.S. Supreme Court. He had not seen any sense in breaking his back on the campaign trail. People already knew who he was, he thought, and campaigning was a waste of energy. After all, a candidate "did not have to be undignified and politically adroit to qualify as head of government," he said.

Hughes went to bed on election night thinking he had won, but when the votes were all counted he had lost the key state of California. He woke up still a Supreme Court justice, not the next president of the United States. It might seem that Hughes lost his chance by not campaigning more vigorously. But in the next presidential campaign, Warren Harding ran with a similar strategy and won the election.

Harding ran against Democrat James Cox. Cox toured tirelessly, making speeches from trains and from the tops of barrels along the main streets of America. Harding, however, stayed close to home, delivering occasional speeches but making no energetic appeals for votes.

SOCIALIST PARTY
FOR PRESIDENT

EUGENE VICTOR DEBS

In 1920, Socialist party candidate Eugene Debs received almost one million votes even though he was in jail during the campaign.

"Why should I tour around the country like Cox when these people all know they can find me at home and will come if they want to see me?" Harding said.

Taking the easy approach, Harding tallied seven million more votes than the hard-working Cox. Even Socialist party candidate Eugene Debs received nearly a million votes that year although he was in prison at the time and unable to truly campaign.

So, is campaigning really important? The answer might be that campaigning *is* important, but that running a presidential campaign is not an exact science. The job can be done in several ways, and no single method guarantees victory. It is almost certain, however, that no candidate could win using Harding's method of passive campaigning today. Any candidate who does not aggressively seek the office is likely to be ignored and, like Charles Evans Hughes, go down in defeat.

The First Modern Campaign

Long ago, people recognized the value of campaigning. In ancient Rome, a candidate's backers would paint information about the man they supported on the city's walls. And in another early form of campaigning, candidates for the Roman Senate would appear before the public wearing what was called a white "gown of humility." The word *candidate*, in fact, comes from the Latin word *candidatus* meaning "dressed in white."

In the United States before the late

1800s, however, it was generally considered bad form to campaign. Instead, candidates left it to their supporters to spread their appeal. They thought candidates should be asked to run by their supporters. The idea was to appear modest and not too eager for power. In 1860, Abraham Lincoln even thought it was improper to vote for himself and he clipped his name from his own ballot before he cast it for other officials.

William McKinley participated in one of the first aggressive, "modern" campaigns. In 1896 he defeated William Jennings Bryan, spending the unheard-of sum of $3,500,000 to do it. In keeping with the old ways, McKinley stayed at home and addressed crowds from his front porch. But he also broke with tradition. He put his campaign in the hands of an expert, a man named Mark Hanna, who is often recognized as the first professional **campaign manager.**

Hanna was a shrewd organizer. Scientific planning, efficiency, and advertising were just being recognized as the way of the future. In keeping with the times, Hanna presented more than just a candidate to voters. He also gave them an "image." Theodore Roosevelt, McKinley's vice presidential running mate that year, recalled,

"Hanna was selling McKinley like patent medicine."

Bryan nearly matched Hanna in flamboyance, if not money. He was among the first candidates to mount a hustling campaign as we know it today: traveling, speaking, and meeting the people. In 14 weeks, Bryan traveled 13,000 miles, making 600 speeches in 29 states. He was an exciting orator and he had a large following among farmers and small-town people. Although he lost the election and his style of campaigning took a while to catch on, Bryan's hectic pace matched against Hanna's crafty "packaging" of McKinley set an example for all future campaigns. Since 1896, presidential campaigns have never been the same.

The first manager of a "modern" campaign, Mark Hanna

5
The Media

In the fall of 1960, then-Vice-President Richard Nixon met Democratic Senator John Kennedy of Massachusetts in a series of four televised debates. Across the country, millions of voters tuned in to see the two presidential candidates go head-to-head, live and unrehearsed.

Both candidates had done extensive research. Both were able to make knowledgeable comments about the issues. But many experts believe Nixon came out the loser in the series, largely because of how poorly he looked in the first of the debates. Kennedy appeared young, exciting, and decisive. Nixon looked tired, poorly shaven, and uncertain. Nixon was recovering from a leg infection that had put him in the hospital. Worse, his face looked shabby because of the poor makeup job he was given before the show.

Opposite: The cameras of the media dominate President John F. Kennedy's view of the crowd during his inaugural speech in 1961. Right: John F. Kennedy and Richard Nixon met for the first televised presidential debates in 1960.

31

Those who heard the debate on radio had a much better opinion of Nixon's performance. In succeeding debates, Nixon was much improved in appearance. But people's first impressions were powerful and lasting. Those impressions were formed on the basis of the candidates' images, not on what either had to say about national policy.

The 1960 debates are a good example of how the **media** — television, radio, newspapers, and magazines — can alter the course of a presidential campaign. The way the media present campaign news may affect how people feel about the candidates. Resourceful candidates can study the ways the media affect voters and use this information to their advantage.

Playing to the Camera

As voters watch any campaign, they should keep firmly in mind the power of the media. Much of what candidates say, where they travel, and how they spend their campaign money, is done with the media in mind.

Television is considered the most powerful of the media. A single television shot allows a candidate to reach millions of people. It is estimated that 65 percent of all voters decide how they will vote for president based on what they see on television.

Further, television has such impact it is sometimes said that "nothing happens until it happens on TV." This means that until a subject is discussed on television, people often don't think of it as "news." Presidential candidates need to appear on television frequently, because if they do not it could be said that their candidacy "hasn't really happened."

Name Recognition

It is easy to see why candidates — especially lesser-known candidates — crave to be seen on television. The most important asset any candidate can have is **name recognition**. That is, have people heard of the candidate? Do they recognize the candidate's face or name? A candidate who does not have name recognition must get it.

In times past, a candidate achieved name recognition only through years of service in public or in party offices, or by having a well-known family name such as Kennedy or Roosevelt. Today, media advisors and lots of money can create name recognition through the media. Candidates no longer need a party organization to help make their names known. They can run their own campaigns through the media.

In 1976, for example, Jimmy Carter began his campaign with almost no name recognition. "Jimmy who?" people said when asked about Carter.

He was the little-known governor of Georgia, and he initially had little backing from leaders in the Democratic party. But Carter traveled extensively, shook a lot of hands, and began to turn up frequently on the news. He won several **primary** elections, the important first round of elections that leads to a party's nomination as candidate. "Jimmy who?" became a popular nickname. The nickname helped Carter's image as the underdog up against the big-name politicians in Washington.

Carter was tagged with another name that year — media candidate. Carter got the name because he was not well known for his work in government but had become well known by using the news media and professional public relations tactics.

Four years later, Carter ran against Ronald Reagan, a former Hollywood actor. Some called it the first presidential campaign between two media candidates. Both Carter and Reagan owed their political careers to the media, and not to a lifetime of political work and connections.

President Jimmy Carter with his wife, Rosalynn, and daughter, Amy

Are the Media too Powerful?

Some people are not happy with the media's influence on campaigns. They argue that television decides for the public who the candidates will be and how successful they will be.

Because the media are not bound to cover all the activities of every candidate, some candidates complain that they are not taken seriously by the media and that they never get the publicity they need. Some say that if, for example, television had ignored Carter's "Jimmy who?" campaign, he might never have made it to Washington.

The media can act as the voters' ally. Politics is complicated, and a voter needs an enormous amount of information to understand all of the issues in a campaign. If voters had to rely on the candidates' speeches and explanations, they could not be sure they were hearing the whole story. After all, candidates want people to hear what will bring votes, not necessarily what is true.

The media give voters information about the candidates' qualifications and character—sometimes information the candidates want to suppress. And they supply voters with information so they can form their own opinions about what the candidates say.

The Media's Shortcomings

Television and radio news time is limited, as is newspaper space. News stories, therefore, are short, quick images with simple explanations. Sometimes a short simple story distorts a complicated issue.

Further, a television network or a newspaper is a business. The way the business makes money is by attracting viewers and readers. Sometimes the media make a big deal out of a small thing in order to create a "story" that people will watch or read about.

Jumping on candidates' mistakes is another way the media may attract attention. When a candidate stumbles in a speech or makes an error in judgment, it is an event people will be interested in knowing more about. Even errors not directly related to a candidate's ability to serve in office interest the voters.

In 1987 Gary Hart, the early favorite for the Democratic nomination in 1988, was reported to have a romantic relationship with a woman other than his wife. The exact nature of the relationship never was made clear, but the media reported Hart's activity as major news. Public discussion was strong enough to force Hart to withdraw from the race. Months after he withdrew, Hart reentered the campaign. But his campaign stalled, largely because of the lingering controversy about his relationship with the woman.

Maybe the biggest criticism the media face is that they report a campaign not as a debate about issues and policies but as a struggle for power. The media rarely present a discussion of the issues or a candidate's political views. Instead, they concentrate on which candidate is "winning" with his or her strategy, style, and wit. The campaign becomes a popularity contest. Voters are encouraged to pick sides in the game, to make a choice by saying,

"I like the candidate" rather than "I agree with the candidate."

Media Campaigns in History

The growth of campaigning in the latter half of the 1800s is closely related to the growth of the media during the same period. Between 1870 and 1890, the number of newspapers sold in the United States doubled, and it doubled again in the next 20 years. The more people a candidate could reach with a speech or appearance, the more sense it made to spend time speaking and making appearances.

Radio was invented and became a campaign tool in the early decades of the 20th century. In the 1924 race, Americans heard campaign speeches on the radio for the first time and for the first time microphones were used at the political conventions.

In 1940, the Republicans presented the first televised political convention. Television was still new, however, and few people owned a set. In 1948, neither party spent any money on television advertisements. Things changed quickly. By 1968, the two parties' total bill for radio and television costs was more than $18 million. And by 1980, about half the budget of each presidential contender went to media and related expenses.

Campaign Commercials

Most of the money a candidate spends on the media is spent on commercials. If given a choice, a candidate most often prefers to appear on the nightly news. After all, an appearance on the news is free, and voters tend to believe what they see on the news more than what they hear in a commercial that was paid for by the candidate. But if candidates are to fully promote their ideas and their image, they must pay for commercial time on television.

In 1952, the Republicans made campaign history by presenting the first political "spot" ads on television. The ads were rehearsed, 60-second commercials in which candidate Dwight Eisenhower responded to questions from actors portraying ordinary citizens. Before 1952, candidates had felt they had to buy half-hour blocks of time to give detailed presentations of their views.

Now almost every major candidate appears on commercials during the campaign.

A relaxed Adlai Stevenson charms a small crowd of supporters during the 1956 presidential race.

6
The Candidate's Staff

In 1952 and 1956, the Democratic Party selected Senator Adlai Stevenson of Illinois as its presidential nominee. Stevenson was a scholarly man and a model of composure. He looked the part of a thoughtful statesman, but sometimes his knowledge made him appear "too smart." His wit occasionally seemed over some people's heads.

In a well-run campaign, Stevenson's strong points would have been accentuated and his weaknesses softened. But in what are considered two of the most poorly run campaigns in recent history, Stevenson lost both races to Dwight Eisenhower.

Because of poor scheduling, he was rushed back and forth around the country, leaving little time for rest or preparation. He arrived at appearances late and out of breath, which undermined his best asset — his sense of composure.

Because of poor research on the part of his staff, he often delivered speeches inappropriate for his audience. The speeches sometimes included punch lines and inside jokes that might have been funny to another crowd, but not to the one he was addressing. Some of his speeches for television were not planned with television in mind. They ran beyond the allotted time, leaving the television audience hanging as Stevenson was cut off the air.

Stevenson's example shows that any presidential campaign is more than the work of a candidate. It takes the effort of a couple of dozen professionals and countless volunteers to plot the strategy, plan the schedules, provide the transportation, and make the phone calls that head the candidate toward the White House. Candidates often discover that good campaign workers can be hard to find for several reasons:

♦ Campaign work is specialized. There is no other job quite like it. Few people are experts in the field.
♦ It is temporary. Anyone who goes to work for a candidate will have to leave another job, and he or she may not be able to get it back if the campaign is unsuccessful.
♦ The pay is low. Often campaign staff work for no pay, with the understanding that if the candidate wins, they will be offered jobs by the new president.

Campaign Chores

The duties of campaign workers differ slightly with each candidate and each campaign. In some cases, one worker may fulfill more than one role, and in other cases the duties of two workers may overlap. These are the standard jobs behind the scenes in a presidential campaign.

Advance People Advance people are staff members who travel to communities ahead of the candidate to prepare for the candidate's appearances. They rent auditoriums, arrange for press conferences and interviews, make hotel reservations, set up local transportation, and organize rallies.

Advance people make sure all of a candidate's events come off smoothly. Any appearance a candidate makes takes an enormous amount of organization from these staffers.

Campaign Manager The campaign manager is the boss of the campaign operation. Even the candidate — the most important person in the campaign — will follow most of the orders the campaign manager gives. The manager, consulting with the candidate and a group of aides, strives to take the candidate's ideas and make them appealing to the largest number of voters.

The campaign manager sets the candidate's schedule. He or she decides the places the candidate should visit and suggests in general what the candidate should say at each stop. The manager, with the help of a media expert, also decides what types of advertisements make the candidate most attractive to voters, and where those advertisements

Campaign staffers meet with the caterers before a fund-raising dinner for Republican Dwight Eisenhower and his running mate, Richard Nixon. Supporters might pay $2,000 each to eat with the candidates at a fund-raising dinner.

should be placed in order to be most effective. It is the manager's job to "sell" the candidate to voters, by judging what qualities the candidate has that voters most want to "buy."

The candidate must have complete confidence in the campaign manager. As a result, the campaign manager is often someone who has been closely associated with the candidate throughout his or her political career. The job requires good organizational skills, a sense of strategy, and expert knowledge of politics.

Finance Director The finance director is in charge of raising funds for the candidate and acting as treasurer for the money received. This is an enormous task because it takes tens of millions of dollars to elect a president.

The finance director will have a strong background in business and accounting and will know the best ways to encourage people to give money to the campaign.

Media Consultant The media consultant coaches the candidate on his or her appearance and manner of speech. The consultant, working with the campaign manager, also advises the candidate about the best

39

Campaign workers might go door to door to hand out literature about the candidate or to ask questions for the poll takers.

ways to be mentioned in magazines and newspapers, on radio and television, and the best ways to advertise for maximum effect. Most modern candidates employ a media consultant at least on a part-time basis.

Pollsters A **poll** is a careful study of how people feel about a certain topic. A pollster asks a small group of people questions, then predicts how the general public would answer the questions based on the answers of the small group.

Poll taking is scientific, and pollsters can be quite accurate in their findings, even though they question only a small number of people. Several well-known organizations conduct regular political polls throughout any campaign. Most presidential candidates still hire their own private pollsters to give them more detailed information than general polls can provide.

Press Secretary The press secretary is the candidate's messenger to the news media. A candidate cannot always be around to talk to reporters. It is the press secretary's job to find answers to key questions and report them back to the press. The press secretary, and his or her staff, writes **press releases**, or summaries of information the candidate wants to tell the press. The press staff also set up press conferences and interviews with reporters, and answer hundreds of telephone calls from the media.

The press secretary must speak well in front of people. He or she must know the issues and know enough about the candidate's positions to answer routine questions on behalf of the candidate.

Research Aides These are the bookworms of the campaign. They do the candidate's "homework," researching facts to help the candidate speak knowledgeably about the issues. Issues constantly change, and so does the public's interest in them. Also, an opponent's claims and charges must be answered by the candidate with supporting facts and figures.

A busy candidate cannot possibly read every newspaper and study every topic. So the research aides keep the candidate up to date, sometimes calling on authorities — professors, lawyers, industry executives — for expert advice.

Speech Writer Candidates rarely take time to write all of their own speeches. Instead, they employ speech writers — sometimes a staff of two or three — to write their speeches.

Although the words may not be written by the candidate, the writers consult closely with the candidate so the speeches always express what the candidate wants to say. Often a traveling candidate speaks several times a day, to people in different cities and with different concerns about the country. The speech-writing staff is always busy.

Volunteer Workers Most of the work in any campaign is done by volunteers. These are the people who stuff envelopes with the letters the candidate sends out asking people to contribute money to the campaign. The volunteers knock on doors in their neighborhoods to spread the word about their candidate. They drive to the airport to pick up a visiting campaign aide or pick up an order of campaign flyers from the print shop. They work for the candidate in their spare time.

Most volunteers are motivated by loyalty, a sense of excitement, and the chance of being rewarded with a job if the candidate wins.

A group of so-called Kennedy "girls"— John F. Kennedy campaign volunteers— awaits their candidate's arrival with great excitement.

In 1912, primary elections had little effect on a party's choice of candidates. Ex-president Theodore Roosevelt (above) won nine state Republican primaries, President William Howard Taft (above right) won one, and Robert La Follette (right) won two. The Republican party chose Taft at the national convention.

7

Primaries and Caucuses

The general presidential election takes place every four years in November, but the race for the presidency officially opens much earlier with the first of the presidential primaries.

In a primary election, candidates of the same party — sometimes as many as 10 or 12 contestants — compete for votes from the people of a particular state. The Democratic candidates, for example, all are trying to become the one Democratic candidate in the general election. The voters cast their ballots for whomever they would like to see represent their party in the general election in November. Democrats vote for Democratic candidates; Republicans vote for Republicans.

By winning votes in a primary, a candidate wins the pledges of **delegates** to vote for his or her nomination at the party's national convention later in the summer. The convention is a meeting of party members from across the country at which the party nominee is officially selected. A *delegate* is a person sent to the convention by the state party organization. Each delegate votes at the convention on behalf of the people of a state.

Traditionally, the first primary election is held in New Hampshire in late January or early February, followed by other early primaries held in Massachusetts, Florida, Illinois, and North Carolina. In the spring or early summer, several big states

— often including California, Ohio, and New Jersey — all hold their primaries on the same day on what is known as "Super Tuesday."

The Caucus Method

During the same period the primaries are being held, some states are holding **caucuses** to choose delegates. Dedicated party members gather at a mass meeting to choose the delegates. Unlike a primary, which is a one-time, mass vote of the public, the caucus method chooses delegates by a mixture of voting and compromise among party members. The rules vary from state to state and by party. The first caucus of an election year is traditionally held in Iowa.

Types of Primaries

There are many different systems of primaries. Some states have **proportional primaries,** in which candidates win delegates in proportion to the number of votes they receive. A candidate who wins two-thirds of the vote, for example, earns two-thirds of the delegates. Other states have **winner-take-all primaries**, in which the candidate with the most votes wins all of the delegates. Still

other states have **advisory primaries**, in which voters' preferences for candidates will later guide those who pick delegates at a state convention or party meeting. These delegates will not be bound to follow the voters' preferences.

In addition, some states have **closed primaries**, in which only registered party members may participate. That is, only voters who registered as Republicans could vote

George McGovern campaigns in a California nursing home during the 1972 Democratic primaries.

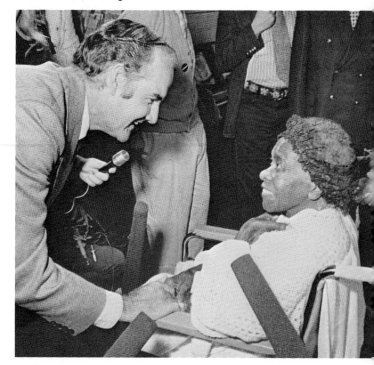

44

in a closed Republican primary. Other states have **open primaries**, in which a voter does not have to be a party member or declare party loyalty and may vote in any *one* party's primary. Still other states have **blanket primaries** in which a voter may vote in more than one party's primary.

The process is complicated even for political experts to understand. The number of delegates and the rules of representation and selection can change each year for each state. Just to make it simple, voters might think of a presidential campaign as a tournament, with the primaries and caucuses being the playoff rounds and the general election being the finals.

Primaries' Hidden Importance

Primaries and caucuses are important to candidates for reasons beyond the delegates they may win. They offer contestants a chance to gain name recognition and to measure their popularity against the popularity of their opponents. Primaries and caucuses test the candidates' strengths and weaknesses.

Some people think primaries emphasize a candidate's style and personal appeal rather than his or her skills as a statesperson. For this rea-son, primaries are sometimes called "beauty contests."

Because the New Hampshire primary and the Iowa caucus usually kick off the campaign season, they are important as media events. They create a **front-runner** or a favorite for the public to follow. The winners make news and immediately increase their national popularity. Their names become more recognizable to more people, they find it easier to raise money, and they find it easier to sway other voters to their side. So although winning in New Hampshire or Iowa means very little in terms of delegates, it means a great deal in terms of media coverage.

The Winner as a Loser

Sometimes the close media attention and the importance of image-making can distort the results of a primary. The process can make a candidate who won seem like a loser.

If the favorite does not win by as large a margin as predicted, for example, the runner-up might be declared the "real" winner because the runner-up gained the most exposure for having made the most unexpected good showing.

In the Democratic primary in New Hampshire in 1968, President

Lyndon Johnson bowed out of the 1968 race when polls predicted he would lose the Wisconsin primary.

Lyndon Johnson got more votes than Senator Eugene McCarthy, but McCarthy was called the "real" winner because he ran a close second and exceeded everyone's expectations. Later, Johnson withdrew from the campaign, and McCarthy became the favorite for the Wisconsin primary. And although McCarthy carried 58 percent of the vote in that primary, it was considered a setback for him because he was expected to earn a greater majority.

Narrowing the Field

After the early primaries, some candidates will decide there is no point in going on with their campaigns. If they do badly in primaries, they know they have lost the interest of the news media and the confidence of their supporters. They will find it hard to raise money for their campaigns, and they will find themselves far behind their competition in the number of delegates pledged to them.

By the time of the national convention, only a few candidates will remain. One candidate might even come to the convention having earned enough delegates to be assured of the party nomination. Or one candidate might have enough delegates to be *nearly* assured of victory. Some candidates with fewer delegates will remain in the race. They are likely to try to trade the support of their delegates for a favor from the front-runner. The favor might be the chance to make an important speech at the convention, a chance at a cabinet position if the party's candidate wins, or even the selection as vice presidential candidate.

History of the Process

Before the 20th century, delegates were either chosen by the caucus method or appointed by powerful state leaders. Voters had little say in choosing the party's candidate.

The first primary election was held in Florida in 1904. The aim was to give every voter who wanted it a chance to take part in the system. By 1912, primaries were used in 13 states, but caucuses remained the most popular method until the 1970s. Powerful politicians did not want to give up their influence by letting the use of primaries spread too far. It remained possible for a candidate to do well in the primaries and still not gather enough delegate support to be nominated at the convention.

In 1968, Senator Eugene McCarthy gathered a great deal of support in the primaries. Vice President Hubert Humphrey had not won a single primary, but he had backing from party leaders in the state caucuses. He won the nomination. The 1968 Democratic convention was torn by violence, however. Much of the protest was against the nomination of Humphrey, who supported the unpopular Vietnam War. Humphrey's nomination was seen as symbol of old-style, unfair politics.

In 1972, the Democrats created a new system using more primaries in the delegate-selection process. The Republicans followed a similar course, and in 1980, 75 percent of the delegates at both conventions were elected by primaries.

The growth of primaries left party leaders almost powerless in the selection of candidates. In 1976, for example, Democratic party leaders would have preferred Humphrey. Jimmy Carter did well in the primaries, however, and won the nomination without the backing of party leaders.

Primary Limitations

Primaries are far from a perfect system for selecting a presidential nominee, and some states have dropped them. In 1980, at least one party in each of 37 states used the primary system. But in 1984, at least one party in each of six states reverted to the caucus method.

One reason is that **voter turnout**, or the number of the registered voters who actually vote, is low in primaries. Primaries rarely bring out more than 30 percent of the voters. Some states believe the public is better served when interested, knowledgeable political people choose the delegates, as in the caucus method.

Right: James Blaine, a Congressional Representative from Maine, almost became the Republicans' 1876 presidential candidate. Below: The Republican national convention cheered when James Blaine finally became their nominee—in 1884.

8

The National Conventions

James Blaine looked like a sure winner of the Republican nomination that night at the 1876 national convention. The speech nominating Blaine had roused the delegates to his side. Blaine's supporters wanted the **balloting** to begin immediately after the speech. Balloting is the process by which nominees are chosen. The delegates vote, and then the votes are counted. If there is no clear winner, then the delegates vote again. Between rounds of voting, supporters of each candidate do their best to convince delegates to switch votes to support their candidate.

However, someone cut the gas pipe and caused the lights to go out in the hall. The balloting did not begin until the next day. Given extra time to organize during the confusion, supporters of Rutherford Hayes pushed their man to the nomination, and Hayes went on to become the 19th president.

The 1948 Democratic convention in Philadelphia was one of the first to be widely seen on television. Its organizers worked hard to put on a show. At a dramatic moment they tried to unleash a covey of pigeons, but the birds would not take flight. Convention workers were forced to toss the birds into the air. The

These 1952 Republican delegates are advertising both their state and their support for Ike (Dwight D. Eisenhower) or Taft (Senator Robert Taft, son of President William Howard Taft).

pigeons went on to rest in strange places and to drop unwanted gifts on delegates. One bird tried to land on convention chairman Sam Rayburn as he addressed the crowd, but Rayburn ducked and the pigeon landed happily on his podium.

What goes on at a national convention of the Democratic or Republican parties sometimes looks like a pep rally, a going-out-of-business sale, and a street party rolled into one. Some speeches draw vicious boos and screams from the crowd, but other speeches no one seems

to listen to. Streamers, banners, and balloons decorate the hall, and the floor is soon littered with paper cups, hot dog wrappers, and discarded campaign literature. A band plays at every unfilled moment, and people dressed in silly hats carry on in the aisles. This is a business meeting?

The Convention's Purpose

One purpose of a convention is to whip up enthusiasm among party members and inspire them to work for the rest of the campaign. Another purpose is to decide the party **platform**. The platform is a statement of the issues the party considers most important to the country, and of how those issues should be addressed.

For example, in 1980, the Democratic party platform contained a plan to spend $12 billion for a jobs program, national health insurance, and education for the poor. They also supported the Equal Rights Amendment (ERA), a proposal many believed necessary to guarantee full rights for women. They officially supported a woman's right to choose an abortion. In addition, the Democrats supported busing as a last resort to achieve racial integration in public schools.

That same year, the Republican platform proposed spending much less than $12 billion for social programs. They officially opposed the ERA and supported a Constitutional amendment banning abortions. In addition, they opposed busing.

The most well-known business of a convention is the nomination of a presidential candidate. But at recent conventions, most delegates reach the convention already pledged to a candidate, and the candidate who will be nominated is often already close to being chosen.

Today, much of the party's business is taken care of before the event and the convention itself can be boring unless something truly unexpected occurs. Modern conventions serve less as a business meeting than as an advertisement for the party and a television spotlight for the politicians who make the speeches.

The Growth of Conventions

Since 1832, all nominations for president and vice president have been determined at conventions. Before the Civil War, national conventions commonly were conducted in small buildings or churches and attracted only a few hundred delegates and few spectators. Today, national conventions are held in large hockey arenas or auditoriums before crowds of thousands and a large television audience.

The Constitution does not require that conventions be held, nor does it say anything about political parties. Early American leaders informally nominated the candidates from among the country's small group of elite politicians. As the country grew to include people in different geographical areas, with differing points of view, political parties grew. The parties were

51

competitive, and they chose their candidates carefully for the maximum chance of victory. This meant the parties had to please a wide range of voters. Thus choosing candidates and making policy grew more complicated.

A small group of political leaders could no longer choose candidates and set policy for party members across the country. So political conventions sprang up as the mass meeting for party members of all types, from all over.

The Convention Schedule

Conventions typically last about a week and include four or five full sessions of business. Among the highlights of a convention is the keynote speech, which is given early in the week, usually by a prominent party member. The keynote speech serves as a welcome, a pep talk, and a call to battle for the party. The party usually asks an exciting, inspiring speaker to make this address.

A day or two later come the nominating speeches, followed by shorter, seconding speeches. Again, these speeches are usually full of political pride and inspiration and are commonly delivered by energetic speakers.

Jesse Jackson gained enough support in the 1988 primaries to help write the 1988 Democratic platform. He also earned an important prime-time speech at the convention.

Sometime during the week the convention delegates will argue about the wording or emphasis of the party platform. The platform will be in the form of a rough draft before the convention, but there may be major additions or deletions by the time the document is completed.

Finally, both the winner of the nomination and the person chosen to be his or her running mate will make speeches accepting their nominations.

52

The Delegates

The process of selecting delegates varies with each state and with each election year. But the number of delegates awarded to each state is consistently based on the size of its population. Texas, for example, sends more delegates to the convention than does Hawaii.

In 1924, the Republicans began a bonus system. States that had supported the party's candidates in the last election can send extra delegates to the next convention. The Democrats started a similar system in 1944.

All 50 states, plus the District of Columbia, Puerto Rico, the Virgin Islands, and Guam, send delegates to the convention. The delegates are usually middle-class citizens who are active in the party politics of their state. They may sharply disagree among themselves about what the party's goals should be, but they are likely to be more committed to the goals of the party than the average Republican or Democratic voter.

Commonly, many of a state's delegates are senators, governors, or other officeholders from that state. Some people believe selecting politicians as delegates hands too much power to those already in power. The Democrats and Republicans each made reforms in the 1970s that have increased the number of members of racial minorities, women, and young people in their state delegations.

Yet fewer and fewer common citizens become delegates. Both parties have changed their policies again to give professional politicians greater influence.

Convention Rules and Credentials

A convention is run according to certain rules, and there is sometimes a battle over the interpretation of the rules and how they should be applied. For example, in 1980 Edward Kennedy urged an **open** convention in which all delegates, even those pledged to a certain candidate, could vote for whomever they chose. Kennedy lost his attempt to overturn the "pledged delegate rule" and lost the nomination to Jimmy Carter.

Another common dispute at a convention concerns the **credentials** of certain delegates. Often two different groups will claim to be their state's "real" delegates, the ones who were rightfully elected to represent their state. The convention then decides which group to approve. Sometimes the approval of one group over another affects the nomination.

In 1912, for instance, 70 Republican delegates who were backers of William Taft were approved over the challenge of a group of Republicans who supported Theodore Roosevelt. Taft went on to win the nomination. When the convention chairman announced the ruling in favor of the Taft delegates, Roosevelt's backers are said to have started yelling, "Choo! Choo! Choo! All aboard! Toot! Toot!," because they believed they had been "railroaded." They eventually walked out of the convention.

Voting for the Nomination

In 1924 it took the Democrats 103 ballots to nominate a presidential candidate. Again and again, the convention chairman called the names of the states in alphabetical order. Over and over, a member of each delegation called out its votes. Neither William McAdoo nor Al Smith could tally a winning margin, so the process would begin again.

Exhausted and frustrated, the Democrats finally decided to compromise. They agreed to nominate John Davis instead of McAdoo or Smith. Davis won just 29 percent of the vote in the general election,

The delegates brace themselves for another round of balloting at the 1924 Democratic convention.

a record low for a Democratic candidate.

Before the Democrats switched to a simple majority system in 1936, candidates in both parties needed a two-thirds majority of votes to win nomination. This made the nomination difficult to win. Many old-time conventions became battlegrounds for votes.

When conventions became hopelessly deadlocked, as the Democratic session did in 1924, often the only solution was for opposing delegates to agree on a compromise candidate. The compromise candidate sometimes was a complete surprise to the public. He was nominated only because he was someone the party could agree upon.

Long evenings of voting and compromise used to be a ritual at conventions, but multiple balloting has become uncommon in recent years. The current primary and caucus systems bind most of the delegates to a candidate long before the voting is done at the convention.

The way in which votes are cast has changed with time as well. At early conventions, voting was informal. At the Democratic convention of 1835, for example, Maryland appointed 188 delegates to cast the state's 10 votes, while the 11 votes for Tennessee were cast by a traveling businessman who happened to be in the convention city at the time. Today, one delegate casts one vote.

Choosing a Running Mate

Some say being vice president of the United States is a boring job. Thomas Marshall, vice president under Woodrow Wilson, put it this way: "Once there were two brothers. One ran away to sea; the other was elected vice president. And nothing was ever heard of either of them again."

A vice president in office may hold much responsibility or little at all. But at convention time, anyone

Until 1804, all candidates ran independently. The winner became president and the runner-up became vice president. In 1800, the House of Representatives had to decide a tie and choose who would be president and who would be vice president.

The House of Representatives chose Thomas Jefferson as president in 1800, and Aaron Burr became his vice president.

mentioned as a candidate for the vice presidency gets a great deal of attention. Once a presidential candidate has been nominated at a convention, attention turns to who will be chosen as the candidate's running mate.

In the country's early years, when there were no formal political parties, each candidate ran for president as an individual. The runner-up for president automatically took the second spot. Then in 1800, Thomas Jefferson and Aaron Burr wound up tied in electoral votes. The election had to be decided by the House of Representatives, and it took them 36 ballots to finally select Jefferson as president.

To avoid further confusion, the 12th Amendment to the Constitution was adopted in 1804. It required that votes be cast distinctly for president or vice president. As political parties sprouted after 1800, candidates began to run as teams sometimes called tickets. Voters then cast their ballots for a party's ticket.

Through most of our country's history, the running mate was selected by the convention or in a meeting of party leaders. Only in 1940 did presidential nominees begin regularly picking their running mates.

That is the year Franklin Roosevelt made Henry Wallace his choice despite the protest of many party members. In recent years, the presidential nominee's preference has carried the most weight, although party leaders and top campaign advisers still are consulted.

Vice presidential candidates are not necessarily chosen for knowledge or policy skills. They are valued most for their ability to **balance** the ticket. That is, the vice presidential candidate should make the ticket appealing to a broad range of people, including people who might not otherwise vote for the presidential nominee.

Vice presidential choices are expected to be loyal campaigners, willing to travel tirelessly and speak with enthusiasm about the party and the ticket. They are also valued for the ways in which they might be different from the presidential nominees. For example, in 1960 Republican candidate Richard Nixon chose Henry Cabot Lodge of Massachussets

In 1964, the convention delegates cheer the Democratic ticket they have just chosen: Lyndon B. Johnson and Hubert H. Humphrey.

as his running mate. Nixon, from California, knew the value of having a person from the East Coast on the ticket. But more important, Lodge was considered slightly less conservative in his views than Nixon.

Although the choosing of a vice presidential candidate seems to be only for show, the choice becomes vitally important if the president should die in office. The vice president then takes over as president.

The Acceptance Speech

Normally the people with a real chance to be nominated for president make themselves scarce at the conventions. For most of the week, they watch television in a hotel room while business goes on at the auditorium.

The night the new nominee is selected, he or she often shows up at the hall to greet the crowd. But it is usually on another night that the candidate and his or her running mate formally accept the nomination. They each make an acceptance speech and, to many people, these speeches are the highlight of the convention.

The custom of delivering the acceptance speech at the convention began in 1932 with Franklin Roosevelt, who flew from New York to Chicago to deliver his acceptance speech. Before Roosevelt, a committee usually was sent to the nominee's home to inform him of his selection, and there, in a public ceremony, he spoke on major issues of the day. The last candidate to accept the nomination in this way was Republican Wendell Wilkie in 1940.

The acceptance speech is not just a few words of acceptance. It has become a chance for candidates to show off their speaking skills, and candidates often try to coin a great slogan that will stick in the public's mind. In his 1932 address, Franklin D. Roosevelt said, "I pledge you, I pledge myself, to a new deal for the American people."

The phrase "New Deal" quickly caught on as a description of Roosevelt's policies, and it has since become the historic title for his presidency.

Homeward and Onward

With the last sounds of the gavel the conventions will end. The delegates will go home with their job completed. For some candidates, the entire presidential campaign will now be about two years old. But it is not over. In some ways it is only beginning.

9
Campaign Spending

Abraham Lincoln's campaign committee spent all of $100,000 to get him elected president in 1860. His opponent, Stephen Douglas, spent $50,000. One hundred years later, Richard Nixon laid out $10,128,000 in a losing cause while the winner, John Kennedy, spent $9,797,000. In 1980, Ronald Reagan and Jimmy Carter each spent more than $29 million in their race for the presidency.

In a modern campaign, candidates need money for airplane travel, food, and hotel bills — not only for the candidate but for dozens of aides

Stephen Douglas (standing behind Lincoln) and Abraham Lincoln met in several debates when they were rivals for the Senate.

Campaign buttons have always been an inexpensive way to advertise the candidate.

and consultants. They need enormous sums to buy commercials on television and ads on billboards and in publications. They need still more money to print campaign literature, buttons, and stickers, and to rent office space for headquarters.

Of course, most of the money is not the candidate's own. Much of it comes from supporters who make donations out of a sense of duty or belief in the candidate, or because they hope to influence the candidate by their generosity. Some of the donations must be used to attract more and larger donations, because a candidate needs a steady stream of income to mount a successful campaign. If candidates can show early in the race that they are popular and have a chance to win, they will find it easier to raise money later. People are more willing to give money to campaigns when they believe the campaign can succeed.

Because campaigning is so expensive, some people say that only rich candidates, or those backed by wealthy people, can win elections. With a lot of money, they say, even a candidate who is not qualified for office can "buy" the election. In reality, candidates of both major parties receive money from many wealthy contributors. It is unlikely that one candidate would far outspend another today, even with a rich family on his or her side.

60

Controlling Campaign Costs

Since the 1970s, politicians have tried to enforce limits on campaign spending. The idea is to allow each candidate to work with equal funds and to slow the never-ending increase as each side tries to spend more money than the opposition. In 1984, for example, candidates were limited to spending $20 million before the conventions and $32 million in the general election.

Another goal has been to limit the amount of money an individual, a company, or an organization can donate to a campaign. When a candidate receives large donations from a certain source, some fear the candidate will play favorites with those who donated heavily to the campaign.

Although Congress passed laws in 1974, 1976, and 1979 to achieve these goals, not everyone agrees that they have succeeded. The laws have

Harry S Truman's whistle-stop campaign in 1948 required money for the special train and for advertising and publicity to gather crowds like this to listen to him.

reduced the importance of having a few large campaign donors and increased the importance of having a large number of small contributors. The laws also require candidates to be more open about where their campaign money comes from and how it is spent.

Under the Fair Campaign Practices Act, major presidential candidates are given equal amounts of public money to use for campaigning. The money comes from a fund that volunteers contribute to when they pay income tax. If they accept the federal money, candidates can spend only $50,000 of their own money on the campaign. But they usually take the federal funds.

Nearly all of the money restrictions can be side-stepped, however, by the use of **political action committees**. Political action committees (PACs) are organizations set up by businesses, labor unions, and other groups to help the campaigns of candidates they like. PACs can spend far more money for a candidate than any group could give in direct contributions. But the money is supposed to be spent without the knowledge or control of the candidate's official campaigns. PACs spent $61 million on candidates in the 1984 presidential campaign.

Modern campaigns also require modern equipment, like computers and photocopiers, for the campaign office.

Clearly, the problem of controlling campaign spending remains. Some suggested solutions have been to put strict ceilings on spending, shorten the campaign period, put a ban on private contributors or PACs, give away free television and radio time to candidates, and have them run their campaigns totally at public expense.

The biggest spender in a campaign usually increases his or her chance of winning. However, money isn't everything. In 1980 John Connally of Texas spent $13.7 million in the presidential race. He had only one delegate pledged to him when he withdrew.

10
Campaign Strategy

For many Americans, Labor Day is a September holiday of picnics and parades. For presidential candidates, it's likely to be the first day back in the public eye after the conventions.

On Labor Day, candidates start back to work, attending four or five holiday events so they will be seen by as many voters as possible. The last holiday of the summer is a valuable chance to greet large numbers of people who have gotten together for relaxation, not politics.

The candidates have not been goofing off since the conventions. One of the first moves candidates will make after the convention is to enlarge their staffs. Workers who had been supporting candidates no longer

Union party candidate William Lemke went to a ballpark in the summer of 1936—to give a campaign speech.

63

in the race have joined the nominee's team. They have brought fresh ideas and maybe some campaign secrets from their former positions.

Together with the new staff members, candidates have been plotting strategy with their staff, setting goals and schedules, and figuring out their strengths and weaknesses. Before the convention, the candidates were running against several opponents within their party. Now the competition has narrowed to only one or two major opponents from other parties. The pace of the campaign begins to quicken and new strategies come into play.

Maintaining Momentum

Way back in the primaries, it was important for candidates to prove their potential to go all the way to the presidency. A candidate who is running ahead of the pack finds it easier to attract more votes.

Later in the race, a candidate must work to keep this **momentum** going. Each candidate therefore spends a lot of time campaigning where he or she is already strong. Likewise, their running mates must campaign where they are already popular.

An old political theory says the key to winning is to simply make sure supporters get out and vote. It is not worthwhile, the theory holds, to try to change the minds of people who do not already support the candidate. The assumption is that voters decide on a candidate early in the campaign.

But candidates cannot ignore large groups of the population. Many politicians now believe they can change a voter's opinion late in the campaign.

In 1980, one poll showed that more than one-fourth of the voters did not decide who to vote for until a week before the election. Further, it showed that Jimmy Carter and Ronald Reagan traded the lead four times before November. This suggests that a well-planned campaign can sway an election and that candidates should try to win votes in unfamiliar territory. They might visit unfamiliar cities and states, and meet with labor or business groups or minority groups that are not considered their allies.

Any success can be helpful. When expectations are low, any new support makes news and adds to a candidate's momentum.

The Electoral College Factor

In 1876, Republican Rutherford Hayes captured 4,036,298 votes and

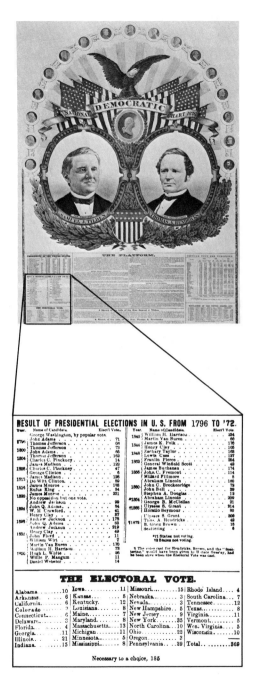

The 1876 campaign banner for Samuel Tilden and Thomas Hendricks showed the electoral vote in presidential elections through 1872 and told how many electoral votes each state had.

won the presidency, even though Samuel Tilden tallied 4,300,590 votes—264,292 more than Hayes. In 1888, Grover Cleveland lost the election to Benjamin Harrison despite capturing 100,456 more votes than Harrison.

How can this happen? It is due to the **electoral college system**.

When people vote for president in the general election, they actually are voting for **electors** from their state who in turn cast their vote for president. The votes cast by electors are called **electoral votes**, and the whole process is called the electoral college system.

Each state has a number of electors equal to the number of its United States senators plus its United States representatives. Each state has two senators, but the number of its representatives is related to the number of people living in the state. More populous states, such as Illinois or Ohio, carry many more electoral votes than smaller states like Delaware or Wyoming. Except in rare cases, the candidate who wins the largest number of popular votes in a state takes *all* of the state's electoral votes. The candidate who wins a majority of electoral votes — not popular votes — wins the election.

A candidate who wins every popular vote in the state of South Dakota wins three electoral votes, but a candidate who wins even by a slim margin of popular votes in California wins 47 electoral votes. So candidates usually do more campaigning in large states where more electoral college votes are at stake.

Third-Party Candidates

In 1912, Republican William Taft might have won a second term as president, but he had a disagreement over policies with fellow Republican Theodore Roosevelt. Roosevelt broke from the Republican party and formed a new party, the Progressive Republican or "Bull Moose" party. Running as a **third-party** candidate, Roosevelt split the Republican vote, taking some of the Republican vote away from Taft. This helped Democrat Woodrow Wilson win.

Third-party candidates are candidates sponsored by any party other than the two major parties, now the Democrats and Republicans. Third-party candidates find it difficult to win in American elections. Only three times has a third party gained enough followers to replace one of the major parties, as the Republicans replaced the Whigs in the 1850s. But the money, power, and tradition in United States politics are firmly behind the two major parties, whichever parties they are.

Third-party candidates can, however, make a mark on the presidential campaign, even if they do not win the presidency. They can attract voters away from one of the major candidates and thereby change the election's outcome.

Campaign Tools

Endorsement   Among the tools a candidate may use in a campaign is **endorsement**. A prominent person or a large, respected institution *endorses* a candidate by saying publicly "We're behind this candidate."

The United Auto Workers, the National Organization for Women, or the Seattle *Post-Intelligencer* newspaper, for example, might announce its support of a candidate. This announcement would send a strong message to thousands of people who respect the opinions of those groups.

Without endorsement a candidate is in trouble, especially if the candidate's own party is reluctant to back him or her. In 1964, Republican candidate Barry Goldwater was considered a weak candidate. Many Republican leaders and candidates refused to appear with him when he campaigned in their states. They did not want to be associated with a "loser." He was defeated by President Lyndon Johnson.

Debate Ronald Reagan earned the nickname "The Great Communicator" and won the 1980 election largely because he was effective in debates with President Jimmy Carter.

Gerald Ford (right) debated Jimmy Carter (left) on television during their 1976 campaign.

Richard Nixon lost the 1960 election partly because he was *not* effective in debates against John Kennedy.

Debating is one of the most powerful, and most risky, campaign tools. Even voters who take only a casual interest in politics pay attention to debates. Candidates who can think on their feet and speak with confidence have a good chance to win votes in a debate. Intelligent, capable candidates who do not communicate well may lose votes.

It was once thought that incumbent presidents should never agree to debate. After all, the president is the president, and a debate allows a challenger to meet the president on equal footing. If the president has a big lead over the challengers, he or she has nothing to gain by agreeing to debate.

In recent years, Presidents Ford, Carter, and Reagan have all debated while they were incumbents. But none of them held a secure lead in the polls. All of them might have thought a debate was a risk worth taking to win.

There are no set rules for how a debate should be presented. Usually more than one debate is scheduled, and each debate is held under slightly different rules and at a different site. This is supposed to even out any advantages for one candidate or another.

Critics of debates argue that the process proves nothing because there is no way to determine who "won." The candidate who shows the most knowledge, for example, may not gain as much from the debate as the candidate who impresses the public with his or her friendliness and sincerity. Further, a good debater does not necessarily have the leadership and decision-making skills to make a good president.

A debate is just a game, critics say, and it should not be used as the only measure of a presidential candidate.

Incumbency In the campaign of 1932, a hitchhiker was said to have carried a sign that read, "Give me a ride or I'll vote for Hoover."

Obviously President Herbert Hoover was an unpopular man in 1932. That November he lost badly to Democrat Franklin Roosevelt.

In most elections, however, the

The economic depression of the 1930s, in which millions lost their jobs, was a big cause of President Herbert Hoover's unpopularity. Right: A line of unemployed men waits to go in to a soup kitchen for a free meal.

incumbent president is the favorite. Fifteen of those seeking a second term have been elected, and only nine have been defeated. The president in office has certain advantages:

- People already know who the president is.
- Whether they like the president or not, people are used to the incumbent's ways.
- Incumbents already have staffs of workers in place.
- Incumbents can claim credit for anything good that has happened in the country during their terms of office.

In addition, the president can use the office to get publicity in ways a challenger cannot. When a baseball team wins the World Series, or someone wins the Nobel Prize, the president can offer congratulations by telephone or before the television cameras. Even the routine parts of the president's job, such as signing a bill into law, can be an excuse for a press conference — and publicity.

Does Strategy Make a Difference?

There are seldom wild swings of public opinion in a campaign. Even a small swing, of course, might be enough to sway an election. Campaign strategy is the candidate's attempt to create that swing, to win over enough voters to make a difference.

Rarely do supporters of one candidate absolutely hate the other candidate. This gives candidates hope that they can persuade the public to change their minds. Studies show, for example, that in 1952, in 1960, and in 1976, most voters perceived *both* candidates in a positive way. The candidates are not always so equal in appeal, however. Most people who voted for Johnson in 1964 disapproved of Goldwater, and in 1972, most Nixon-backers disliked McGovern intensely.

Perhaps the trickiest factor in plotting campaign strategy is knowing that voters never actually receive a candidate's campaign message clearly. People filter what they see, forget what they hear, and bend what they learn about a candidate. This is only natural when dealing with people's opinions. And it explains why surprises still can happen in a presidential campaign.

11
Campaigning on the Issues

Despite the use of imagery, gimmicks, and advertising in political campaigns, not everything campaigning politicians say is just hot air. Sometimes candidates discuss the real issues that face the country. Sometimes they are even prepared to take a stand that offends some voters.

Usually, being frank is dangerous. Most often it is wiser for a candidate to speak in general terms and not make specific statements that are easy to challenge. A candidate who speaks vaguely about the issues is not necessarily stupid. On the contrary, because many problems are complicated and difficult to solve, the candidate who offers neat, easy solutions to them may be the fool.

However, candidates can appear to make an important statement or take a strong stand without actually doing so. A candidate may declare, for example, that he or she is opposed to "wasteful spending" deplores "crime" and supports "prosperity" and the "American way."

A voter might ask, who is not opposed to wasteful spending and crime? Who does not support prosperity and the "American way"? By repeating these phrases, candidates give voters something they can agree with. Candidates who can get voters to agree with them can get their votes.

Opposite: William Jennings Bryan's campaign poster shows his position on trusts and other issues of 1900.

Knowing the Issues

Even if they cannot solve the nation's problems, all presidential candidates must have a solid knowledge of current issues.

A candidate from Boston cannot study only the problems of big cities. He or she must be able to talk to voters about land use and conservation in order to win votes in the Western states. Likewise, a candidate from Montana cannot stick to issues like mining and forestry.

James K. Polk ran for president in 1844 on a pledge to add Texas to the country and to settle a dispute with Great Britain over Oregon.

He or she must be knowledgeable about business and labor problems in order to win votes in the large Eastern cities.

Issues and Elections

In many campaigns, one national issue overshadows the rest. This pivotal issue is the one voters consider the most important. How the candidates stand on that issue means more to the voters than the candidates' personal appeal, experience, and other factors.

1844: Expansion   In 1844, the big issue was frontier expansion. James Polk defeated Henry Clay over whether the United States should aggressively seek to add to its land boundaries. Polk believed in expansion, and by 1848, Texas had been admitted to the union and California, Arizona, New Mexico, Nevada, Utah, and part of Colorado were United States land.

1860: Slavery   In 1860, the big issue was slavery. The Democratic party split over this question, nominating one candidate in the North and one in the South. This split and Republican Abraham Lincoln's comparatively moderate views about slavery helped

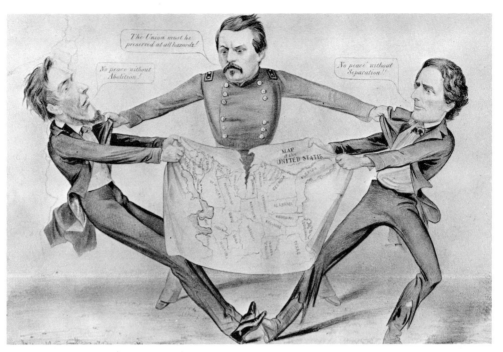

Slavery and abolition were still the issues in 1864. This cartoon shows General McClellan trying to keep Abraham Lincoln (left) and Jefferson Davis (right) from tearing the country apart over the issue of slavery.

him win the election. The issue of slavery was so strongly felt that voters who disagreed with Lincoln's position caused their states to secede, or withdraw from the union. This disagreement led directly to the Civil War.

1932: Economy In 1932, the big issue was the economy. When elected in 1928, President Herbert Hoover had promised "a chicken in every pot and a car in every garage." But the stock market had "crashed" on "Black Thursday," October 24, 1929. The prices of stocks had fallen to a small fraction of their value the day before. Many people had bought stocks which were now worth much less than they had paid for them. Businesses lost so much money that they closed. More than 15 million workers lost their jobs. By 1932, Hoover could only promise voters that "Prosperity is just around the corner."

Franklin Roosevelt's policies sounded new and appealing to the voters in 1932.

1968: War In 1968, a major issue was the Vietnam War. President Lyndon Johnson had said when he was elected in 1964 that he would not send "American boys 9,000 or 10,000 miles away from home to do what Asian boys ought to be doing for themselves." But United States troops had been sent to fight anyway.

Many Americans opposed the war. As America sent more and more soldiers to Vietnam, with no end to

United States Marines in South Vietnam near the Laotian border. The Vietnam War caused more protest than any other war in American history.

Hoover's solution for recovery was "rugged individualism." If government stayed out of the way, he believed, private business could recover by itself. Democratic candidate Franklin Roosevelt, however, believed government should act to bail out failing industry.

The American voters were ready for a change, and Roosevelt won by a large margin. His administration started many programs such as Social Security, which has the government pay money to the poor, disabled, and elderly. He expanded the range of the government's responsibility for individuals.

the war in sight, more and more people grew impatient with the conflict. Some people marched with signs or refused to serve in the armed forces. Some of the demonstrations against the war became violent.

The fight for the Democratic nomination divided the party. Eugene McCarthy, an anti-war candidate, lost to Vice President Hubert Humphrey. Humphrey supported the Vietnam War out of a sense of loyalty to the President. He won the nomination at the convention, but was rejected by people who opposed the war. Humphrey eventually rejected the

Wherever Humphrey spoke in 1968, protesters arrived to demonstrate against the war.

National Guardsmen stand guard against antiwar protesters outside the convention hall during the 1968 Democratic convention in Chicago.

President's war policy, but too late to help his campaign.

With the Democrats splintered by bitterness over the war, Richard Nixon won the presidency by a call to "law and order" in American cities and "peace with honor" in Vietnam.

Nixon's "peace with honor" policy meant that America should seek to leave Vietnam, but not without first turning back the enemy, the North Vietnamese. During Nixon's administration, America's involvement in Vietnam increased. In 1974,

75

the U.S. troops finally left Vietnam. The North Vietnamese were not defeated.

Uniting the Voters

A candidate's campaign promises will become the policies of the new government if the candidate is elected. Does it matter on election day what the candidates really think about the issues? Many political experts think it does not. It is more important, these experts say, for candidates to talk about subjects in ways that encourage large numbers of people to find agreement among themselves.

Candidates who express their exact feelings on a topic risk angering many voters. That's because it is difficult for large numbers of people to agree on very specific subjects. Ask a million people, for example, if they like to eat corn on the cob with butter. Many would say no. Ask the same people if they like to eat corn prepared any way they choose. Many more people would be able to say yes. Further, ask the same people if they like to eat vegetables of any kind. Even people who don't like corn at all could answer yes.

In the same way, candidates are better off building support among people who agree on general subjects, like vegetables. They will be less successful if they try to convince all people on specifics, like corn on the cob with butter. Without the votes of people who only partially agree with them, candidates cannot win election to office. If they are not in office, they cannot work on any of the policies they might really believe in.

Even if elected, a president must obtain the approval of Congress each time he or she wants to make a meaningful change. Here again, a president must make compromises in what he or she might really believe in order to govern. The president's private thoughts about an issue become almost unimportant. It is more important for him or her to lead people of different opinions to an agreement than to try to impose his or her personal views on the public.

12
Mudslinging

"If you can't stand the heat, get out of the kitchen," President Harry Truman liked to say.

It is appropriate advice for presidential candidates. Almost every campaign runs on criticism between opponents and charges from the press. Any candidate whose feelings are easily hurt must think again about running for president, because the name-calling and accusations can get ugly. Andrew Jackson was called a murderer, a gambler, and an adulterer. Abraham Lincoln was ridiculed as a fourth-rate lawyer.

Historically, close races have been especially likely to turn into **smear** campaigns. Candidates might say almost anything to smear or tarnish their opponents' reputations.

This summarized the experience of the two 1968 vice presidential candidates. The ad ended with: "Think the unthinkable. 'President Agnew?'"

President Grover Cleveland married Frances Folsom in the White House on June 2, 1886.

At other times criticism has been harsh but playful. President Grover Cleveland received some of this kind when he was renominated by the Democrats in 1888. During his first term he had married a woman not half his age. Some people did not approve of the marriage, and one newspaper wrote, "Our President evidently has more of an eye for a shapely ankle than for some pressing matters of state."

Whatever most voters thought about his marriage, Cleveland was not reelected. Republican candidate Benjamin Harrison became the next president.

Dealing with Criticism

When faced with harsh criticsm or an unfounded charge, there are several responses a candidate can make. He or she might:

Deny It   Soon after the Republican convention in 1952, opponents charged vice presidential candidate Richard Nixon with wrongdoing. They said he had accepted gifts from wealthy California bankers while he served in Congress, gifts which might have been bribes. Presidential nominee Dwight Eisenhower urged Nixon to answer the charges, saying Nixon's vice presidential spot was on the line.

Nixon spoke on television — in itself an unusual move for a politician in the 1950s. In a half-hour speech, he denied the charges, saying he had not used any of the money or gifts in question for himself. With his wife Pat alongside as he spoke, Nixon mentioned that she wore not an expensive mink coat, but a "respectable Republican cloth coat." He went on to say he had accepted only one personal gift — a cocker spaniel named Checkers, who also was shown on screen. Nixon's children so loved Checkers, Nixon said, that "regardless what they say about it, we're going to keep it."

Nixon's talk was effective in turning public opinion to his side. It is credited with saving his spot on the ballot. Since then it has been known as the "Checkers speech."

Ignore It If a candidate believes his or her campaign is strong, especially if he or she is an incumbent, the candidate may try to stay above the battle when dirt is thrown and not get involved in the **mudslinging**.

President Ronald Reagan, for example, was accused by opponents in 1984 of being too old and in failing health. His opponent, Walter Mondale, was a vigorous man in his 50s who had been in politics over 20 years. Reagan faltered during their first televised debate. He seemed hesitant and mentally confused, and he had trouble holding onto a train of thought. Mondale emerged as the winner of that debate, and when they met again, Reagan only managed a tie. But when asked about the age issue, Reagan responded, "I am not going to exploit for political purposes my opponent's youth and inexperience."

Richard and Pat Nixon with daughters Julie (left) and Tricia. This photo was taken about 12 years after the Checkers speech.

Counter It In the 1952 campaign between Republican Dwight Eisenhower and Democrat Adlai Stevenson, the Republicans followed Stevenson with a "Truth Squad." Whenever Stevenson said anything the Republicans felt was wrong or misleading, they responded by answering his remarks in the local media.

Admit It In addition to the controversy over his marriage, President Grover Cleveland was accused of being the father of a child whose mother he had not married. In

Cleveland's time, fathering a child outside of marriage was scandalous.

The charge came, as many charges do, during the very last days of the campaign when there was little time for Cleveland to answer the accusation. Although Cleveland was not sure if he was the child's father, he told the press he was. He thought it was the best way to minimize any damage to his campaign.

File a Complaint Candidates can always file complaints about questionable campaign tactics with the Fair Campaign Practices Committee in Washington, D.C. The committee is not powerful, however, and reporting an incident is good only for its publicity value. Usually, the committee merely makes a public announcement of the original charge along with the opponent's denial. The committee does not say which side is in the right.

The Truth as a Smear

At a routine press conference during the 1972 campaign, Democratic vice presidential nominee Thomas Eagleton said he had been admitted three times to hospitals in the 1960s for nervous exhaustion, depression, and fatigue.

Eagleton's medical history was not a lie spread by others. It was the truth. But even as truth it was damaging. Democratic leaders and presidential nominee George McGovern decided that voters would react negatively to the news. Eagleton withdrew from the race.

After Eagleton withdrew as a vice presidential nominee in 1972, McGovern lost badly to President Nixon. Some thought the Eagleton incident a major reason why McGovern lost. They said it was not Eagleton's medical history but the way the Democrats handled the situation that lost the campaign. By hastily changing vice presidential nominees, the Democrats looked indecisive, disorganized, and insensitive to people who have been treated for psychological problems.

13
After the Election

President-Elect Andrew Jackson on his way to Washington to take office in 1829.

A winning presidential candidate is called the **president-elect** until he or she takes office in January. For a few months, the next president can savor the victory without the responsibility. And he or she can look back on a long and difficult struggle to reach this point.

The road to the White House probably began over a year before the election, when the candidate began putting together the campaign staff, raising money, and striving for publicity. With some luck, the candidate achieved strong name recognition with the voters. Then the actual struggle for the party's nomination began with the New Hampshire primary in January or February. An exhausting round of primaries and caucuses lasted until June, and by then the party's nomination was probably sewed up. At the national convention in the summer, the delegates voted as they were pledged, and the nomination was final. Then the candidate chose a running mate, made the acceptance speech, and left the convention on a wave of support.

The candidate had time to draw a deep breath after the convention, and then came the *real* race. The strategy was changed and refined as the candidate focused on the opponents in the other parties rather than his own. Another exhausting round of speeches, appearances, and strategy sessions led up to the vote on election day. The candidate's workers put out one last big effort to make sure all of their supporters voted, and it worked. The voters had come through. The electoral college's choice was just a formality.

Now the president-elect is being looked at closely once again. Many voters who were critical of the candidate during the campaign will try now to find things to like about him or her. The president-elect will be examined about matters of business. Voters will want to know who he or she will choose as aides and advisers. A new president must decide whom to appoint to the president's cabinet.

During the period of changeover, the president-elect will be briefed by the outgoing president. The business of paying the bills of the campaign and closing the campaign offices and accounts is going on in the background. And, of course, the president-elect and his or her staff have a big celebration to plan for the inauguration.

Unsuccessful candidates are awarded no office or duty as a consolation prize. They pay the bills of their campaign, thank their supporters, and head home to resume private lives. They might disappear from view for the rest of their careers. Or they might begin to plan for the next election, four years away.

On a brisk January day, the new president will swear a solemn oath to uphold the Constitution. Then he or she will begin what many believe to be the toughest job in the world.

President Nixon and his wife, Pat, on the Great Wall of China. Nixon made some important changes in United States policies, like reopening relations with China. He also was caught in a major scandal during his term of office and was forced to resign.

Chart of the Presidents

	President	Served	Vice President	
1.	George Washington	1789-1797	John Adams	(1789-1797)
2.	John Adams	1797-1801	Thomas Jefferson	(1797-1801)
3.	Thomas Jefferson	1801-1809	Aaron Burr	(1801-1805)
			George Clinton	(1805-1809)
4.	James Madison	1809-1817	George Clinton	(1809-1812)
			Elbridge Gerry	(1813-1814)
5.	James Monroe	1817-1825	Daniel D. Tompkins	(1817-1825)
6.	John Quincy Adams	1825-1829	John C. Calhoun	(1825-1829)
7.	Andrew Jackson	1829-1837	John C. Calhoun	(1829-1832)
			Martin Van Buren	(1833-1837)
8.	Martin Van Buren	1837-1841	Richard M. Johnson	(1837-1841)
9.	William H. Harrison	1841	John Tyler	(1841)
10.	*John Tyler	1841-1845		
11.	James K. Polk	1845-1849	George M. Dallas	(1845-1849)
12.	Zachary Taylor	1849-1850	Millard Fillmore	(1849-1850)
13.	Millard Fillmore	1850-1853		
14.	Franklin Pierce	1853-1857	William R. King	(1853)
15.	James Buchanan	1857-1861	John C. Breckinridge	(1857-1861)
16.	Abraham Lincoln	1861-1865	Hannibal Hamlin	(1861-1865)
			Andrew Johnson	(1865)
17.	*Andrew Johnson	1865-1869		
18.	Ulysses S. Grant	1869-1877	Schuyler Colfax	(1869-1873)
			Henry Wilson	(1873-1875)
19.	Rutherford B. Hayes	1877-1881	William A. Wheeler	(1877-1881)
20.	James A. Garfield	1881	Chester A. Arthur	(1881)
21.	*Chester A. Arthur	1881-1885		
22.	Grover Cleveland	1885-1889	Thomas A. Hendricks	(1885)
23.	Benjamin Harrison	1889-1893	Levi P. Morton	(1889-1893)
24.	Grover Cleveland	1893-1897	Adlai E. Stevenson	(1893-1897)
25.	William McKinley	1897-1901	Garret A. Hobart	(1897-1899)
			Theodore Roosevelt	(1901)
26.	*Theodore Roosevelt	1901-1909	Charles W. Fairbanks	(1905-1909)
27.	William H. Taft	1909-1913	James S. Sherman	(1909-1912)
28.	Woodrow Wilson	1913-1921	Thomas R. Marshall	(1913-1921)
29.	Warren G. Harding	1921-1923	Calvin Coolidge	(1921-1923)
30.	*Calvin Coolidge	1923-1929	Charles G. Dawes	(1925-1929)
31.	Herbert C. Hoover	1929-1933	Charles Curtis	(1929-1933)
32.	Franklin D. Roosevelt	1933-1945	John N. Garner	(1933-1941)
			Henry Wallace	(1941-1945)
			Harry S Truman	(1945)
33.	*Harry S Truman	1945-1953	Alben W. Barkley	(1949-1953)
34.	Dwight D. Eisenhower	1953-1961	Richard M. Nixon	(1953-1961)
35.	John F. Kennedy	1961-1963	Lyndon B. Johnson	(1961-1963)
36.	*Lyndon B. Johnson	1963-1969	Hubert H. Humphrey	(1965-1969)
37.	Richard M. Nixon	1969-1974	Spiro T. Agnew	(1969-1973)
			+Gerald R. Ford	(1973-1974)
38.	#Gerald R. Ford	1974-1977	@Nelson A. Rockefeller	(1974-1977)
39.	James E. Carter, Jr.	1977-1981	Walter F. Mondale	(1977-1981)
40.	Ronald W. Reagan	1981-1989	George H.W. Bush	(1981-1989)

*Took over the office upon the death of the president
#Took over the office upon the resignation of the president

Chart of the Presidents

	Political Party	Occupation or Profession	Runner-Up	
1.	None	Planter	John Adams	(1789, 1792)
2.	Federalist	Lawyer	Thomas Jefferson	(1796)
3.	Democratic-Republican	Planter, lawyer	Aaron Burr	(1800)
			Charles C. Pinkney	(1804)
4.	Democratic-Republican	Lawyer	Charles C. Pinkney	(1808)
			De Witt Clinton	(1812)
5.	Democratic-Republican	Lawyer	Rufus King	(1816)
6.	Democratic-Republican	Lawyer	Andrew Jackson	(1824)
7.	Democratic	Lawyer	John Quincy Adams	(1828)
			Henry Clay	(1832)
8.	Democratic	Lawyer	William H. Harrison	(1836)
9.	Whig	Soldier	Martin Van Buren	(1840)
10.	Whig	Lawyer		
11.	Democratic	Lawyer	Henry Clay	(1844)
12.	Whig	Soldier	Lewis Cass	(1848)
13.	Whig	Lawyer		
14.	Democratic	Lawyer	Winfield Scott	(1852)
15.	Democratic	Lawyer	John C. Fremont	(1856)
16.	Republican	Lawyer	Stephen A. Douglas	(1860)
			George B. McClellan	(1864)
17.	National Union	Tailor		
18.	Republican	Soldier	Horatio Seymour	(1868)
			Horace Greeley	(1872)
19.	Republican	Lawyer	Samuel J. Tilden	(1876)
20.	Republican	Lawyer	Winfield S. Hancock	(1880)
21.	Republican	Lawyer		
22.	Democratic	Lawyer	James G. Blaine	(1884)
23.	Republican	Lawyer	Grover Cleveland	(1888)
24.	Democratic	Lawyer	Benjamin Harrison	(1892)
25.	Republican	Lawyer	William J. Bryan	(1896, 1900)
26.	Republican	Author	Alton B. Parker	(1904)
27.	Republican	Lawyer	William J. Bryan	(1908)
28.	Democratic	Educator	Theodore Roosevelt	(1912)
			Charles E. Hughes	(1916)
29.	Republican	Editor	James M. Cox	(1920)
30.	Republican	Lawyer	John W. Davis	(1924)
31.	Republican	Engineer	Alfred E. Smith	(1928)
32.	Democratic	Lawyer	Herbert Hoover	(1932)
			Alfred M. Landon	(1936)
			Wendell L. Wilkie	(1940)
			Thomas E. Dewey	(1944)
			Thomas E. Dewey	(1948)
33.	Democratic	Businessman	Adlai E. Stevenson	(1952, 1956)
34.	Republican	Soldier	Richard M. Nixon	(1960)
35.	Democratic	Author	Barry M. Goldwater	(1964)
36.	Democratic	Teacher	Hubert H. Humphrey	(1968)
37.	Republican	Lawyer	George S. McGovern	(1972)
			(no election)	
38.	Republican	Lawyer	Gerald R. Ford	(1976)
39.	Democratic	Businessman	James E. Carter, Jr.	(1980)
40.	Republican	Actor	Walter F. Mondale	(1984)

+Sworn in upon resignation of vice president
@Sworn in to replace Ford who became President on August 9, 1974

For Further Reading

Bailey, Thomas A. *Presidential Saints and Sinners.* New York: Free Press, 1981.

Gray, Lee Learner. *How We Choose a President.* 5th ed. New York: St. Martin's Press, 1980

Hoopes, Roy. *The Changing Vice-Presidency.* New York: Thomas Y. Crowell, 1981.

Kronenwetter, Michael. *The Threat from Within: Unethical Politics and Politicians.* New York: Franklin Watts, 1986.

Morris, Richard B. *The Founding of the Republic.* Minneapolis, Minnesota: Lerner Publications Company,1985.

Raber, Thomas. *Election Night.* Minneapolis, Minnesota: Lerner Publications Company, 1988.

Samuels, Cynthia K. *It's a Free Country! A Young Person's Guide to Politics & Elections.* New York: Atheneum, 1988.

Vaughan, Harold Cecil. *The Hayes-Tilden Election of 1876: A Disputed Presidential Election in the Gilded Age.* New York: Franklin Watts, Inc., 1972.

Important Words

The terms listed below are defined on the indicated page:

86

Index

Acknowledgements

The illustrations are reproduced through the courtesy of: Bill Fitz-Patrick/The White House, p. 2; Independent Picture Service, pp. 6, 12, 42 (top left), 59, 60, 74 (top); Library of Congress, pp. 8, 9, 10, 14, 26, 29, 42 (top right), 48 (both), 54, 65 (both), 68 (left), 70, 72, 73, 78, 81; U.S. Signal Corps (Brady Collection), National Archives, p. 15; Dwight D. Eisenhower Library, pp. 16, 22; Defense Nuclear Agency, p. 17; Gerald R. Ford Library, p. 18; Minnesota DFL Party, pp. 19, 40, 41, 57, 62; John F. Kennedy Library, p. 25; Labadie Collection, University of Michigan Library, p. 28; U.S. Army, p. 30; Southdale-Hennepin Area Library, pp. 31, 50, 75 (bottom); Jack Kightlinger/The White House, p. 33; Minnesota State Historical Society, p. 36; Mahoney/Wasserman & Associates for Hilton Hotels in Hawaii, p. 39; State Historical Society of Wisconsin, p. 42 (bottom right); United Press International, pp. 44, 46, 67; National Rainbow Coalition, p. 52; The Collection of the Corcoran Gallery of Art, p. 55; Bowdoin College Museum of Art, Brunswick, Maine, p. 56 (left); The Collection of the New Jersey Historical Society, p. 56 (right); AP/Wide World Photos, p. 61; National Archives, p. 62; U.S. Information Agency, National Archives, p. 68 (right); Cpl. M. C. Patterson/U.S. Marine Corps, p. 74 (bottom); Minneapolis *Tribune*, p. 75 (right); Gordon Twiss, p. 77; Nixon-Agnew Headquarters, p. 79; The White House, p. 83